Rock Music Library

Jim Morrison

by Michael Burgan

CONSULTANT: MEREDITH RUTLEDGE
ASSISTANT CURATOR
ROCK AND ROLL HALL OF FAME AND MUSEUM
CLEVELAND, OHIO

Capstone press

Mankato, Minnesota

Edge Books are published by Capstone Press
151 Good Counsel Drive, P.O. Box 669, Mankato, Minnesota 56002
www.capstonepress.com

Library of Congress Cataloging-in-Publication Data
Burgan, Michael.
    Jim Morrison / by Michael Burgan.
    p. cm.—(Edge Books. Rock music library)
    Includes bibliographical references and index.
    ISBN 0-7368-2702-1 (hardcover)
    1. Morrison, Jim, 1943–1971—Juvenile literature. 2. Rock musicians—United
States—Biography—Juvenile literature. [1. Morrison, Jim, 1943–1971. 2. Musicians.
3. Rock music.] I. Title. II. Series.
ML3930.M68B87 2005
782.42166'092—dc22   2003026402

Summary: Traces the life, career, and impact of rock musician Jim Morrison.

Editorial Credits
Angela Kaelberer, editor; Jason Knudson, series designer; Molly Nei, book designer;
    Jo Miller, photo researcher; Scott Thoms, photo editor; Eric Kudalis, product
    planning editor

Photo Credits
Corbis, 18; Corbis/Bettmann, 17, 21; Henry Diltz, 5, 9, 22
Getty Images/Hulton Archive, cover; Tim Mosenfelder, 27
Michael Ochs Archives, 14
Patrick D. Dentinger, 25
WireImage/Chris Walter, 6, 13; James Fortune, 10; Kevin Mazur, 28

1 2 3 4 5 6 09 08 07 06 05 04

Table of Contents

CHAPTER 1

Rock and Roll Star

On May 10, 1968, about 15,000 fans filled a Chicago arena. They cheered as Jim Morrison stepped on stage and began to sing. Jim was the lead singer and main songwriter for the Doors.

Jim led the Doors as they played their hit songs. These songs included "Break on Through," "Five to One," and "When the Music's Over."

Jim did more than sing the words to the songs. He performed as if he were acting in a play. Sometimes he fell to the stage and pretended he was in pain. Then, he leaped up and jumped into the air. Later, Jim ripped off his shirt and threw it into the crowd.

Learn about:

A powerful performer

Poet and musician

Early death

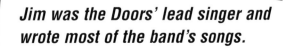

Jim was the Doors' lead singer and wrote most of the band's songs.

Jim was both a musician and a poet.

The Doors finished with two encores, then left the stage. The crowd stood and called for the band to play more. Some of the fans rushed onto the stage. Jim had stirred strong feelings in the fans who loved him and his music.

A Talented and Troubled Artist

With the Doors, Jim was one of the most popular performers in rock music. Jim wrote both poetry and song lyrics. Many of his poems and songs were about love, death, or other personal topics. Other lyrics dealt with war or problems in society.

Young Americans during the 1960s often questioned rules set for them by adults. Jim and the Doors shared many of those feelings.

Jim was intelligent and talented, but he had problems with drugs and alcohol. His drug and alcohol abuse often hurt his ability to work. It also may have led to his early death. Jim was only 27 when he died. Fans still wonder what great songs and poetry he might have written if he had lived longer.

CHAPTER 2

Early Years

Jim Morrison was born December 8, 1943, in Melbourne, Florida. He was the oldest child of Steve and Clara Morrison. Steve served in the U.S. Navy. The Morrisons moved often while Jim was growing up. Clara did most of the work raising Jim, his brother, Andy, and his sister, Anne.

Jim was always interested in words. He wrote his first poems when he was in grade school. Jim read many books. He liked poems and stories by writers involved in the beat movement. These writers included Jack Kerouac and Allen Ginsberg. Jim sometimes wrote poetry in the style of the beat writers.

Learn about:

Childhood

Moving to Los Angeles

Forming the Doors

Jim loved to read and had a large collection of books.

Jim decided he wanted to learn to make movies.

High School and College Years

In 1958, Jim's family moved from Alameda, California, to Alexandria, Virginia. In high school, Jim received good grades without studying much. He often wrote poems and personal thoughts in a notebook.

Jim enjoyed telling shocking stories. He once told a teacher he had to miss a class because he was having an operation on his brain. Some classmates thought Jim was a little odd. Still, he was popular.

After high school, Jim went to St. Petersburg Junior College in Florida for one year. Then he attended Florida State University (FSU) in Tallahassee. He studied poetry and philosophy. Jim also acted in several plays. But what he really wanted to do was make films. Jim decided to leave FSU and study film in California.

"There were so many sides to Jimmy. You'd see one, then get a glimpse of another. You never knew what he was thinking."
—Caroline Morrison, Jim's grandmother

Starting the Doors

In 1964, Jim entered the University of California at Los Angeles (UCLA). He met another film student, Ray Manzarek. Ray played keyboards in a band.

In June 1965, Jim graduated from UCLA. Later that summer, he saw Ray on a beach. Jim told Ray he had written some songs.

Ray loved Jim's songs. He asked Jim to join a band he had formed with his brothers. The group was called Rick and the Ravens. They were joined by drummer John Densmore. By late 1965, Ray's brothers had left the group. Guitar player Robby Krieger replaced them.

The band changed its name to the Doors. The name came from a poem by William Blake. The poem says the "doors of perception" must be clean for people to understand the world. Aldous Huxley used the poem for the title of his book *The Doors of Perception*. This book was a favorite of Jim's. Jim wanted the band to help people learn about themselves, as well as about life.

The Doors were (clockwise from top left) Ray Manzarek, Jim, Robby Krieger, and John Densmore.

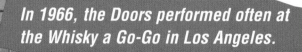

In 1966, the Doors performed often at the Whisky a Go-Go in Los Angeles.

Early Success

By early 1966, the Doors were performing in small nightclubs in Los Angeles. The band often played at the Whisky a Go-Go. The Doors played before better-known groups came on stage.

Jim first drank alcohol and used illegal drugs in college. His alcohol and drug use sometimes affected his performances. The manager of the Whisky a Go-Go fired the band because of Jim's behavior.

Losing their job at the Whisky didn't seem to hurt the Doors. The band had many fans who were attracted to the music and to Jim's lyrics. Soon, the Doors signed a recording contract with Elektra Records. The band began to record its first album.

"I was just taking notes at a fantastic rock concert that was going on in my head."
—Jim Morrison, describing how he wrote songs

CHAPTER 3

Rising Star

The Doors released their first album in January 1967. It was called *The Doors*. The album featured some of Jim's songs as well as some by Robby Krieger. Jim insisted that the entire band take credit for writing the songs. He also said the money the band earned should be split evenly.

The Doors' first hit single was the song "Light My Fire." The success of the song and the album made the Doors huge stars. They won praise from rock music writers and played in front of larger crowds.

Learn about:

Success with the Doors

Drug and alcohol problems

Jim's last days

The Doors' first album made them huge stars.

Jim continued to write and perform songs that appealed to young people.

Becoming Famous

The Doors soon started work on their second album. *Strange Days* came out in October 1967. The song "Hello, I Love You" reached number one on the charts.

The third Doors album was *Waiting for the Sun*. It came out in July 1968. A song called "Unknown Soldier" was about the Vietnam War (1954–1975). At the time, many young people were protesting the war.

Inside the album cover was Jim's poem "Celebration of the Lizard." Part of it said, "I am the Lizard King/I can do anything." Jim said lizards and snakes were related to the forces of evil. Jim wanted to explore both the good and evil in people and the world. Some people began to call Jim the "Lizard King."

Edge Fact
Jim wrote "Celebration of the Lizard" as a song. It was 24 minutes long when recorded. The band didn't want to fill half the album with only one song. They decided instead to print the poem on the inside of the album cover.

Troubled Times

Jim's success didn't seem to make him happy. He continued to use illegal drugs. He drank even more alcohol. Twice, he was arrested at concerts for creating a disturbance.

In early 1971, the Doors recorded a new album, *L.A. Woman*. The band had not had a major hit song in more than two years. The songs "Love Her Madly" and "Riders on the Storm" brought the Doors back to the top of the music charts.

After the album came out, Jim left Los Angeles. He and his girlfriend, Pamela Courson, moved to Paris, France. No one knew if he would ever perform again with the Doors.

In 1969, Jim and his lawyer went to court after one of Jim's arrests.

L.A. Woman *was Jim's last album.*

A Mysterious Death

In Paris, Jim hoped to focus on his writing. He had published several books of poetry. Jim wanted to write more poetry and perhaps a novel.

Jim learned that *L.A. Woman* was doing well. He called drummer John Densmore and said he might want to record another album with the band.

John was the last member of the Doors to speak to Jim. On July 3, 1971, Pamela found Jim dead in their bathtub. Some people believe he had taken illegal drugs the night before. A French doctor said he had died from natural causes. Later, Jim's friends could not find this doctor. Three years later, Pamela died of a drug overdose. The truth about how Jim died is still not known.

CHAPTER 4

Jim's Impact on Music

Jim's death added to his image as a mysterious, troubled person. Some people believe Jim faked his death and is still alive. But most people accept that Jim is dead. Thousands of fans have visited his grave in Paris.

In 1971, the Doors recorded a new album without Jim. Writers at *Rolling Stone* magazine hated it. The band's next album received a better review. But the Doors were not the same without Jim. The band broke up.

Learn about:

Continued popularity

Impact on today's music

The Doors of the 21st Century

Each year, thousands of people leave flowers at Jim's grave in Paris.

Shaping Rock and Roll

Rock fans continue to buy the albums Jim recorded with the Doors. They also buy new recordings of the band's greatest hits and live concerts. In 1993, the band was inducted into the Rock and Roll Hall of Fame.

Over the years, the Doors' music has influenced many bands. These groups include Creed, Days of the New, and Pearl Jam. U2 sometimes works parts of Doors' songs into their live performances.

In 2000, several bands recorded a collection of Doors songs. The CD *Stoned Immaculate* features bands such as Stone Temple Pilots and Creed. These groups wanted to honor the influence Jim and the Doors had on their music.

Pearl Jam

Pearl Jam helped define the grunge sound of the early 1990s. Bass player Jeff Ament and guitarist Stone Gossard formed Pearl Jam in 1990 in Seattle, Washington. Guitarist Mike McCready, drummer Dave Abbruzzese, and singer Eddie Vedder soon joined the band.

Pearl Jam's first album, *Ten*, came out in 1992. Rock critics and fans heard the influence of Jim Morrison and the Doors in the band's powerful songs "Alive," "Jeremy," and "Black." In 1993, Vedder sang with the remaining Doors members at a ceremony honoring the Doors' induction into the Rock and Roll Hall of Fame.

Ray Manzarek and Ian Astbury are two members of the Doors of the 21st Century.

The New Doors

In 2002, Robby Krieger and Ray Manzarek formed a new version of the Doors. They called the band the Doors of the 21st Century. Ian Astbury became the band's lead singer. Astbury had been the lead singer of the Cult.

The new band did not play all the old songs. One song they chose not to do was "The End." Jim wrote "The End" early in the band's career. The song dealt with death and a story from ancient Greek myths. Robby said it would not be right to play "The End" without Jim.

Fans welcomed the chance to hear other Doors songs in concert. For a moment, they could close their eyes and pretend Jim was still on stage.

Glossary

album (AL-buhm)—a collection of music recorded on a CD, tape, or record

charts (CHARTS)—lists that show how many people buy a certain CD, tape, or record

encore (ON-kor)—a song played after a band ends the main part of a concert

lyrics (LIHR-iks)—the words of a song

myth (MITH)—a story told by people in ancient times; myths often tried to explain natural events.

perception (pur-SEP-shuhn)—an understanding of the world through the senses of sight, smell, touch, taste, and hearing

recording contract (ri-KOR-ding KON-trakt)—a legal agreement between a record company and a band

Read More

Gish, D. L. *Rock 'n' Roll.* World of Music. North Mankato, Minn.: Smart Apple Media, 2002.

Hayes, Malcolm. *1960s: The Age of Rock.* 20th Century Music. Milwaukee: Gareth Stevens, 2002.

Lewis, Jon E. *Jim Morrison.* They Died Too Young. Philadelphia: Chelsea House, 1998.

Internet Sites

FactHound offers a safe, fun way to find Internet sites related to this book. All of the sites on FactHound have been researched by our staff.

Here's how:
1. Visit *www.facthound.com*
2. Type in this special code **0736827021** for age-appropriate sites. Or enter a search word related to this book for a more general search.
3. Click on the **Fetch It** button.

FactHound will fetch the best sites for you!

Index